Plas Newydd

ISLE OF ANGLESEY

A souvenir guide

Ymddiriedolaeth Genedlaethol
National Trust

CW00351853

A FAMILY HOME SHAPED BY LOVE AND WAR

Old and new

Plas Newydd means 'new mansion', but its history is actually far from new. It stretches back over 5,000 years to the Neolithic cromlech (burial mound) on the lawn by the stables. The superb views of Snowdonia across the Menai Strait make this the perfect place for a house, and there has been one here since at least the early 16th century.

The story of Plas Newydd has a rich cast of characters, driven by the contrasting passions of love and war.

The careful courtier

The Pagets acquired Plas Newydd by marriage in the 18th century, having first established themselves on the national stage during the reign of Henry VIII. William, 1st Baron Paget (1505/6–63) was a loving husband and a cautious diplomat, who somehow survived the perilous world of Tudor court politics.

'One-leg'

Henry, 1st Marquess of Anglesey (1768–1854) was the greatest British cavalry officer of his generation. He was awarded his title (and his nickname) for his bravery at the battle of Waterloo in 1815, where he served under the Duke of Wellington and lost a leg (the remains were amputated without anaesthetic). This did not stop him fathering a further ten children by his second wife, Charlotte Wellesley, with whom he had eloped in 1810. To complicate matters further, she was the Duke's sister-in-law.

The proud performer

The 5th Marquess of Anglesey (1875–1905) built his own private theatre at Plas Newydd to indulge his obsession with the theatre. Having spent a fortune on lavish jewellery and costume, he died young and bankrupt in 1905.

Passion in paint

The 6th Marquess of Anglesey (1885–1947) rescued Plas Newydd from his spendthrift cousin and brought it into the modern age, installing *en suite* bathrooms and rejuvenating the garden in the 1930s. He also commissioned Rex Whistler's famous Dining Room mural. This romantic fantasy landscape is full of illusionistic tricks and private family jokes. Whistler also painted many portraits of the 6th Marquess's eldest daughter, Lady Caroline Paget, to whom he was devoted. He died tragically young, while fighting in France in 1944.

Plas Newydd renewed

The present Marquess inherited the estate in 1947, and has devoted much of his energies to reviving the garden after the inevitable neglect of the Second World War. He is the author of the definitive history of the British cavalry, in which his great-great-grandfather served with such distinction, and has supported numerous good causes, private and public, in Wales and beyond. In 1976 he generously gave Plas Newydd to the National Trust and continues to live here with his family.

Above Lady Caroline Paget; painted about 1938 by Rex Whistler, who was devoted to her

Left The Battle of Waterloo (detail); painted by Denis Dighton. Lord Uxbridge (later 1st Marquess of Anglesey) appears prominently on the right

Opposite The east front at dawn

THE CHANGING FACE OF PLAS NEWYDD

The Tudor house The earliest surviving fragment of the original house is a stone doorway in the basement which is probably early 16th-century. The Music Room also began life around this date, as a late medieval great hall, with a chapel to the north.

Early 1750s Inspired by Wales's great Plantagenet fortresses such as Conwy and Beaumaris, Sir Nicholas Bayly transformed Plas Newydd from a house into a castle by adding battlements and semicircular and octagonal towers. This is an early, if fanciful, example of the Gothic Revival style (Bayly seems to have acted as his own architect). It is entirely appropriate that the central tower should have been christened 'Mount Rascal'.

1782–6 As soon as Henry Bayly, 1st Earl of Uxbridge inherited the estate, he called in a local architect-mason, John Cooper of Beaumaris, to make improvements. Cooper added another octagonal tower at the north-east corner to balance that at the south-east.

1793–9 Lord Uxbridge turned to the fashionable architect James Wyatt, who had already built country houses in the Gothic style and – more controversially – had also drastically restored some of Britain's finest medieval cathedrals. From the start, Wyatt worked with Joseph Potter, a Lichfield joiner who had earlier assisted him at Hereford and Lichfield cathedrals. Wyatt was notoriously busy and disorganised, so Potter took on increasing responsibility for the project. He completely reorganised the west range of rooms, replaced the Great Hall with the spacious Music Room, and inserted the Gothick Hall and a new staircase at the north end of the house. However, circulation within the house remained poor, and it was still not obvious where the front door was.

1805 Potter returned to add a new wing to the north containing servants' quarters on the ground floor and a chapel above. The house was rented out or left empty for much of the 19th century, and little was done to the fabric.

Below The East Front in 1770; by Moses Griffith

Right The East Front c.1790

Right The East Front c.1800 (detail); by John 'Warwick' Smith
Below The East Front in 1806; by Moses Griffith

1913 The 6th Marquess completely redecorated the interior.

1919 Electric lighting was installed in the house and the stables.

1920s The 6th Marquess abandoned the Pagets' ancestral family home, Beaudesert in Staffordshire, bringing much of its contents to Plas Newydd.

1922 The architect Owen Little was asked to modernise the house. He improved the servants' quarters, but died in 1931 before the work could be completed.

1930s The architectural historian and architect Harry Goodhart-Rendel proposed an ambitious scheme to remove many of Plas Newydd's Gothick features and Georgianise the exterior, some of which was carried out. He concentrated on making the interior more comfortable with a new dining room and library, and more bedrooms and bathrooms.

Right The East Front c.1800 (detail); by John 'Warwick' Smith

Below The East Front in 1806; by Moses Griffith

The 6th Marquess rejects Goodhart-Rendel's more radical proposals

'I am now quite convinced that we must avoid everything which brings a new note into the elevations of the house. Our only chance of making something agreeable is slavishly [to] copy the spirit of the existing house – it has never been an architecturally correct house and we can never make it one.'

THE APPROACH

THE DAIRY (TEA-ROOM)

The u-shaped, single-storey Dairy was probably designed by Joseph Potter about 1810. It comprises a tiled milking parlour in the centre (now the National Trust tea-room) and two wings, which now house the shop and toilets.

THE STABLES

You first catch sight of the Stables from the Dairy across the wide expanse of lawn. The west façade, with its Gothic windows, battlements and turrets, is easily mistaken for the house itself – a mistake often made with British country houses, where horses can be almost as grandly accommodated as their owners. It was built by Joseph Potter in 1797, perhaps to designs by James Wyatt, whose work it resembles. It was intended to house fourteen horses and two carriages. The work was supervised by the 1st Earl of Uxbridge's friend and neighbour, Lt-Col William Peacocke of Plas Llanfair, who also advised on the garden (see p.29). In the 1930s the Stables (not open to visitors) were the base for the 6th Marquess's successful bloodstock breeding business.

Below The Stables

THE CROMLECH

To the left of the Stables stand five large boulders, which together once formed a cromlech (the burial chamber of a Neolithic chieftain). It is one of the best preserved such monuments on the island of Anglesey, despite the attentions of 18th-century antiquarians, who removed its original covering of earth in the fruitless hunt for signs of Druidic human sacrifices. During one of his visits to Plas Newydd in the 1790s to advise on the garden, Humphry Repton expressed concern that this ancient burial site had been 'lately endangered by wanton mischief'.

Above The cromlech

THE WEST (ENTRANCE) FRONT

The Gothick charm of the late 18th-century house was somewhat spoilt in the 1930s by the 6th Marquess, who removed the battlements and added a wall at right-angles to the house to screen out parked cars from the garden. Whistler designed the flamboyant doorways in the wall. Four slender octagonal turrets survive, together with three tall Gothic sash-windows, which light the grand Music Room. There are two entrances – both quite modest – one each side of the screen wall: a slightly awkward arrangement.

THE EAST (STRAIT) FRONT

Sir Nicholas Bayly's 1751 south-east corner turret is balanced at the opposite, north-east corner by another octagonal turret, which was added in 1782–6 by John Cooper. Bayly's semicircular bay dominates the centre of this front. The 6th Marquess shortened the flanking turrets, simplified the windows and created the long Dining Room, which now displays Rex Whistler's mural.

THE NELSON BLOCK

The large wing attached to the north end of the house was designed in 1805 as service quarters, which were considerably altered and extended in the mid-1930s. During the Second World War, the Merchant Navy training ship HMS Conway moved here from Birkenhead to escape enemy bombing. In 1949 the training school moved into the Nelson Block and the Stables, where it remained until the mid-1960s. In 1968 Cheshire County Council took over the Nelson Block as an Outward Bound centre for Cheshire children. The interior has been adapted over the past 60 years for institutional use, but the external fabric remains little altered.

Above The West (Entrance) Front in 1939; painted by Rex Whistler, who appears in the foreground. The present Marquess is riding the bicycle on the path below. Whistler designed the wall at right-angles to this front, which screens the car-park from the garden

TOUR OF THE HOUSE

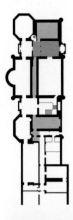

THE GOTHICK HALL

With its gallery and fan-vaulted ceiling, this is a fine example of a late 18th-century Gothick interior. It looks as though it is made of stone, but – typically for the Gothick style – the ceiling is actually painted plaster and the columns are wood. The room (completed in spring 1797) was the work of the Lichfield joiner Joseph Potter, who had assisted James Wyatt in restoring the cathedral in that city.

Left The Gothick Hall, with the Music Room beyond

Pictures

On the right-hand wall hang three portraits of the Tudor courtier *William, 1st Baron Paget* (1505/6–63), who founded the family fortunes, but never lived at Plas Newydd. The best version is the largest – in the centre. On the wall opposite is Van Dyck's sensitive full-length portrait of *Katherine Manners, Duchess of Buckingham* (*c*.1603?–49). A wealthy and shrewd businesswoman 'of great wit and spirit', in 1620 she married for love James I's favourite, the 1st Duke of Buckingham (murdered in 1628), and became one of the most influential women at the court of Charles I.

On the wall to the right of the entrance door is *Caroline Paget* (d.1766), whose marriage to Sir Nicholas Bayly in 1737 united the Paget and Bayly families and ultimately brought her family's heirlooms to Plas Newydd.

'We, for a short time, imagined ourselves in a chapel.' A visitor in 1828

What is Gothick?

The Gothick style was the first phase of the Gothic Revival, especially popular among British antiquarians between about 1720 and 1830. It was inspired by the pointed arch of medieval architecture, but was more delicate and romantic and less archaeologically correct than the Victorian Gothic Revival style. In the 1930s Rex Whistler revived the Gothick spirit in creating murals like that in the Plas Newydd Dining Room.

Furniture

The mahogany *hall chairs* were decorated with the coat of arms used by Caroline Paget's son, Henry Bayly, between 1770 (when he became 9th Baron Paget) and 1784 (when he was created Earl of Uxbridge). Hall chairs were deliberately kept simple, as they had to be hard-wearing.

Sculpture

The small 18th-century *alabaster busts* on the right-hand table are of the Italian medieval poets Petrarch and Dante.

Banners

The crimson silk banners were carried by the Royal Horse Guards, and are embroidered in silk with the battle honours this cavalry regiment (now the Blues and Royals) won during the Peninsular and Waterloo campaigns.

Left The hall chairs are decorated with the coat of arms of the 9th Baron Paget (later 1st Earl of Uxbridge)

THE MUSIC ROOM

This was the site of the Great Hall in the 16th-century house. Around 1796–8 it was transformed and enlarged by Potter to its present appearance for the music-loving 1st Earl of Uxbridge. Potter was probably following designs by Wyatt, who had created a similar-looking chapel for Magdalene College, Oxford. The plasterwork ceiling with its ornate bosses (painted a Portland stone colour in 1913) and the medieval knights in the chimneypiece niches were intended vaguely to evoke the spirit of medieval hospitality. Even the sash-windows were given pointed tops.

The room has been used ever since for large-scale entertainment and to display the best of the family portraits.

Below *The future 1st Marquess of Anglesey* (detail); by John Hoppner and Sawrey Gilpin, 1798

Pictures

The very large portrait on the left-hand side of the entrance wall depicts the 1st Marquess of Anglesey, aged about 30, as colonel of his cavalry regiment, the 7th Light Dragoons (later 7th Hussars). He had already gained a reputation for his military prowess and as a dandy. The Marquess was painted by John Hoppner, and his mount by the specialist horse painter, Sawrey Gilpin. The Marquess appears again over the fireplace about 20 years older as the hero of Waterloo, painted in 1817 by the greatest portraitist of the era, Sir Thomas Lawrence. To the right of the fireplace is the 1st Marquess's first wife, Lady Caroline Villiers, with their eldest son, Henry. The couple's divorce in 1810 was a notorious Regency scandal (see p.42). To the left of the fireplace is the Marquess's eldest sister, Lady Caroline Capel, who was in Belgium during the Waterloo campaign: 'To have one's friends walk out of one's Drawing Room into Action, which has literally been the case on this occasion, is a sensation far beyond description'.

A portrait of the 1st Marquess's father, the 1st Earl of Uxbridge, hangs in the centre of the far wall. He is dressed in his peer's robes. The old Houses of Parliament (destroyed by fire in 1834) are in the background. Lord Uxbridge appears in a smaller portrait to the right of the door.

A birthday party for George IV, August 1821

'Tables were laid the entire length of that noble apartment and ... what attracted the chief notice of the delighted guests was the confectionery which was displayed in an endless variety of ornaments, distributed with infinite taste throughout the several tables.'

Lighting

On the window wall are four silver-plated wall-lights made in the [1920s] for electricity, but in the style of Charles II wall-sconces. They came from the Long Gallery at Beaudesert and, like the *light-switches* throughout the house (shown above), they are decorated with the 6th Marquess's coronet. They resemble wall-lights in the Long Gallery at Haddon Hall, a Derbyshire family home of the 6th Marquess's wife, Lady Marjorie.

Right The Music Room

THE STAIRCASE HALL

The main stairs were originally at the south end of the house, but were moved here in the 1790s. In contrast to the Gothick Hall and Music Room, this room and the others you will see are decorated in the Neo-classical style. The Doric columns on the landing and framing the window are wood painted to resemble green *verde antico* marble. The work was supervised by Potter, who supplied the wrought-iron and partly gilt bronze staircase balustrade with its elegant anthemion (honeysuckle) decoration. The staircase itself was probably designed by a draughtsman in the Wyatt office. The plaster walls were painted to resemble finely cut stone in 1913.

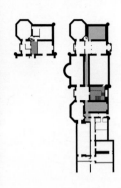

Carpet
The Wilton stair carpet was laid in 1914, but had worn out by the mid-1990s, when it was replaced by a replica, made in Bulgaria.

Patent
Under the stairs is the original 1553 document whereby Edward VI granted William Paget his peerage as 1st Baron Paget.

Pictures
Around the lower walls are episodes from the Duke of Marlborough's wars in the early 18th century. They were copied from murals by Louis Laguerre that once decorated Marlborough House in London. Among the battles depicted are Blenheim, Ramillies and Malplaquet.

Top left The Duke of Wellington was painted in 1840 aged 72 by John Lucas, who (according to the Duke) had 'made the best portraits of me since Lawrence'

Left The Prince Regent; studio of Thomas Lawrence

John Lucas's full-length portrait of *the Duke of Wellington* over the stairs was commissioned in 1840 by the 1st Marquess, who had long wanted to possess a portrait of the Iron Duke, but had been prevented by 'certain political events' (i.e. the Marquess's divorce: his second wife had previously been married to the Duke's brother). They were eventually reconciled, and were to be seen walking arm-in-arm round the 1851 Great Exhibition.

The portrait of *the Prince Regent* (later George IV) was painted in the studio of Sir Thomas Lawrence in 1814. The Prince loved dressing up in uniform (he is depicted as a field marshal, although he never actually served in the army). He envied the 1st Marquess his slim figure, but was very fond of him, declaring in 1815 that 'he *loved* him … he was his best officer and his best subject'. In 1820 the Marquess served as Lord High Steward at the Prince's coronation.

Flanking the Prince are full-length portraits thought (despite the labels) to be of *Sir Nicholas Bayly* and his wife, *Lady Caroline Paget*.

THE MIDDLE LANDING

This passage runs along the spine of the house, widening at the centre to form a top-lit lobby, which provides access to rooms in the middle tower.

Pictures

John 'Warwick' Smith's now sadly faded *watercolours* record how Plas Newydd and Beaudesert looked around 1800. On the right-hand wall hang black chalk drawings of the 1st Marquess's seven children by his first wife. The most notorious was **Lord William Paget** (1803–73), an incorrigible spendthrift who ended up in Marshalsea debtors' prison, causing his father continual anguish: 'I am shocked, disgusted, shamed, at all I hear! What a catalogue of meanness ....'

13

Above Lord William Paget, the black sheep of the family

THE GOTHICK HALL GALLERY

From here you get a good view of the Gothick Hall's ceiling vaults and of the *The Butcher's Stall* and *Bear Hunt* by Frans Snyders (1579–1657). The doors have been painted to resemble mahogany.

Left The Staircase Hall
Right The Gothick Hall Gallery

THE DRESSING ROOM

Pictures

The eight-year-old girl is **Lady Florence Paget**, youngest daughter of the 2nd Marquess. Nicknamed 'The Pocket Venus', she was to be the sensation of the 1863 season, when she caught the eye of Henry Chaplin. They were engaged the following year, but at the eleventh hour she had a change of heart, slipping away from Marshall & Snelgrove while trying on her trousseau to elope with the 4th Marquess of Hastings. Alas, the couple did not live happily ever after: Hastings gambled away his fortune and died young.

The present Marquess's aunt, **Lady Winifred Paget, Viscountess Ingestre**, was painted with her son (later the 21st Earl of Shrewsbury) by J.J. Shannon, an artist much favoured by the Manners family, from which the 6th Marquess's wife came.

Charles, 6th Marquess of Anglesey created Plas Newydd as we see it today, commissioning the Dining Room mural from Rex Whistler, who began this portrait about 1937, but never completed it.

Right Lady Florence Paget, 'the Pocket Venus'; painted by Henry Graves

Below Lady Marjorie Manners, later Marchioness of Anglesey; by Jacques-Emile Blanche

LADY ANGLESEY'S BEDROOM

This bedroom has been used by successive Marchionesses of Anglesey for at least a hundred years. It occupies the first floor of the octagonal tower built in 1753 by Sir Nicholas Bayly. Facing south-east, it receives the best of the morning sun, but there are also good views north towards the Britannia Bridge.

Decoration

The chimneypiece and frieze date from Potter's and Wyatt's remodelling of the 1790s. Lady Marjorie devised the present pink and white colour scheme in the 1930s with the guidance of the fashionable interior designer, Sibyl Colefax. It is now somewhat faded, but the floral chintz fabrics, Mauny lace wallpaper (replaced by the National Trust), kidney-shaped dressing table

Sibyl Colefax

'In decoration and gardening, she always chose the cooler tones, the simpler flowers.'

Harold Nicolson

and fitted carpet are an atmospheric and important survival of the period.

Furniture
Flanking the four-poster bed are *Rococo mirrors* in the style of Thomas Chippendale.

Pictures
The portrait of *Lady Marjorie Manners*, who used this room, was painted by Jacques-Emile Blanche in 1909, three years before she married the 6th Marquess.

Right Lady Anglesey's Bedroom

LADY ANGLESEY'S BATHROOM
In the 1930s the 6th Marquess led the way in bringing new levels of comfort to the traditionally spartan British country house. He installed central heating, modern plumbing (including numerous *en suite* bathrooms) and fitted carpets.

'Every bathroom should have a bedroom'

The 6th Marquess of Anglesey

LORD ANGLESEY'S BEDROOM

The present Marquess (like his father before him) used this as his bedroom until he gave the house to the National Trust in 1976.

The frieze and the white and Siena marble chimneypiece were installed in the 1790s.

State Bed

The magnificent State Bed has what is known as a 'flying tester' – that is, the canopy appears to be weightless, but is actually supported from the ceiling. Created about 1720, the bed is covered with Chinese silk painted with flowers that matched Chinese wallpaper in the State Bedroom at Beaudesert, where it originally stood. The silk was badly damaged by water used to put out a fire at Beaudesert in 1909. So when the bed was brought here in the 1930s, it was in a reduced form, and minus its curtains, which were turned into matching window pelmets. If you look up into the canopy, you will see the best preserved sections of the material.

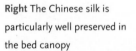

Right The Chinese silk is particularly well preserved in the bed canopy

Pictures

The group of largely 19th-century *marine paintings* reflects the family's love of the sea and Plas Newydd's coastal setting.

Furniture

The *travelling dressing case* to the left of the bed is one of the few pieces at Plas Newydd that survives from the era of the 5th Marquess, whose reckless extravagance ended in a 40-day sale in 1905 (see p.45).

Carefully descend the spiral staircase and cross the rear of the Gothick Hall to reach the Ante-room.

Left Lord Anglesey's Bedroom

Below The spiral staircase

THE ANTE-ROOM

The doors open out onto the lawn, from which there are superb panoramic views across the Menai Strait to the mountains of Snowdonia.

The plasterwork and the double-doors date from the 1790s, the metal Crittall windows and vivid blue walls from the 1930s.

Pictures
The portraits are of the 1st Marquess's father and of his younger brother, the Hon. Berkeley Paget (by Lawrence).

Furniture
The painted chair was upholstered in the 1930s with *toile de Jouy* fabric, which was also used on the suite in the Octagon Room.

What is *toile de Jouy*?

The technique of printing designs from copper plates onto cotton furnishing fabric, usually in a single colour, was pioneered in Britain (this example was made by Robert Jones in 1769). However, today it is always known as *toile de Jouy*, after the factory founded in 1760 by Christophe-Philippe Oberkampf at Jouy-en-Josas on the southern outskirts of Paris, which produced the most famous examples. It became fashionable once again in the 1930s as part of the Georgian Revival.

Right In the Octagon Room, *The Menai Bridge*; painted by George Arnald in 1828, two years after the bridge was completed

THE OCTAGON ROOM

This room was probably created in the early 1750s and was always one of the main living rooms in the house. Lady Anglesey used it as her sitting room (her bedroom was conveniently placed immediately above).

The white marble fireplace was supplied in 1795 by the sculptor Richard Westmacott the elder, who often worked with James Wyatt. The vivid scarlet walls recall the most famous octagonal red room in the world – the Tribuna of the Uffizi in Florence.

Doors
The double-doors to the Ante-room are fitted with 'sympathetic hinges', which enable you to open both doors at once while pushing only one. This ingenious device was invented by James Wyatt's brother Samuel. (*The door mechanism is very old. Please do not try to close it.*)

Pictures
Over the chimneypiece is a view of the **Menai Bridge**, the masterpiece of the engineer Thomas Telford and the longest suspension bridge in the world when it was completed in 1826.

Flanking the fireplace hang photographs of the present Marquess and his sisters in dungerees, taken about 1924 and 1930.

Ceramics
On the mantelpiece is displayed French Samson porcelain from the late 19th century, imitating the style of *c*.1770.

Bronzes
On the games table are a **statuette of the 1st Marquess** as a general of hussars by William Theed, and a copy of Canova's **bust of**

Napoleon. Canova's gigantic full-length nude statue of Napoleon in marble is now at Apsley House, the Duke of Wellington's London home.

Furniture
The furniture is mainly of the Regency and George IV periods. The chairs are upholstered in more of the nautical *toile de Jouy* pattern to match the curtains and pelmets.

Above A *toile de Jouy* armchair
Below The Octagon Room

THE SALOON

This is the main sitting room, with fine views over the Menai Strait from the large bay window. It was added to the house in 1751 by Sir Nicholas Bayly, who called it 'the great room'. By 1802 it had become the Saloon. Wyatt designed the frieze of flower garlands and the mahogany double-doors in 1795. Wyatt's door surrounds have gone, as have the Chinese silk wall-hangings, which were given to the family by Queen Charlotte.

In the 1930s the 6th Marquess transformed the room by introducing four large pastoral scenes, together with the comfortable sofas and the fitted Wilton carpet.

Below The Saloon

Pictures

The pastoral landscapes, which were originally at Beaudesert and two of which are dated 1789, were painted by the Flemish artist, Balthasar Paul Ommeganck (1755–1826). Ommeganck had a highly successful career painting scenes of peasant life bathed in a warm Italian sunlight, usually on a much smaller scale.

Over the fireplace is Richard Barrett Davis's *Queen Victoria riding out in Windsor Great Park*, 1839. Riding behind her on the grey is the Earl of Uxbridge (later 2nd Marquess of Anglesey), who was then Lord Chamberlain at Queen Victoria's court.

Sculpture

On the marble plinths in the bay window are bronze busts by Sir William Reid Dick of Marjorie, Marchioness of Anglesey (1925) and her daughter, Lady Caroline Paget (1923).

Opposite Ommeganck's four large pastoral scenes dominate the Saloon

THE BREAKFAST ROOM

This room had gained its present name by 1842. In the 1920s it was being used as a smaller, secondary dining room. Wyatt and Potter redecorated the room in the 1790s with a frieze similar to those in the Octagon and Ante-room.

REX WHISTLER (1905–44): MASTER MURALIST

Whistler demonstrated a facility for drawing at a very young age. An important early influence was the 18th-century landscape of classical temples, columns and grottoes at Stowe in Buckinghamshire, where his younger brother Laurence (who later revived the art of glass-engraving) was a pupil. He studied at the Slade School of Art, where his talents were recognised by Prof Henry Tonks, who in 1926 recommended him to decorate the restaurant at the Tate Gallery. His murals on the theme of *The Pursuit of Rare Meats* were an instant success, admired for their charm and assured sense of colour and composition. Whistler was taken up by fashionable aesthetic society and became one of the leading 'Bright Young Things' of the 1930s. Unlike many of his circle, he was immensely productive (partly because he needed to earn a living). Drawing on the decorative language of the early 18th-century Rococo style and the dreamy mood of artists such as Watteau and Boucher, he created an entirely personal vision of the world, which he applied to a bewildering variety of different projects large and small.

Whistler's output included further murals for private houses like Plas Newydd; portraits of the Paget family; set designs and programmes for stage and cinema; book illustrations and dust jackets; *toile de Jouy*-style patterns for chintz and Wedgwood bone china; posters, caricatures, book-plates, Christmas cards and even luggage labels.

At the outbreak of the Second World War, Whistler could have become an official war artist, but instead decided to join the Welsh Guards, which provided further surprising outlets for his fertile artistic imagination. He was killed in Normandy in July 1944 during his first hours in action. He was not yet 40.

Whistler's work can also be seen at Clandon Park in Surrey, Mottisfont Abby in Hampshire and Dorneywood in Buckinghamshire. It has been much imitated, but never bettered.

23

Above Rex Whistler included a self-portrait in the Plas Newydd murals

Opposite The Plas Newydd conversation-piece; begun by Whistler in 1938 and never completed. Lady Caroline Paget leans against the doorway of the Music Room. The present Marquess paints at the easel. Lady Rose reads. The 6th Marchioness plays the piano, watched by her daughters, Lady Mary and Lady Katharine. The 6th Marquess is seated in the armchair

Left
Rex Whistler's paint box

'He saw the world with the eyes of another age'.

Osbert Sitwell

MARJORIE

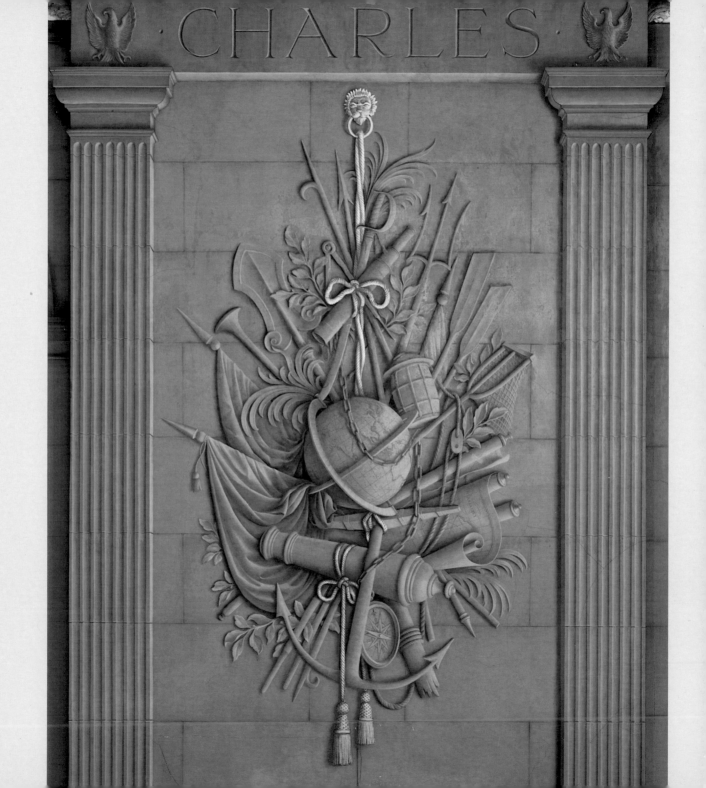

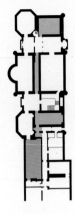

THE WHISTLER DINING ROOM

The 6th Marquess created this long formal dining room in the 1930s from what had previously been housekeeper's and footmen's rooms.

Making the mural

The idea of asking Whistler to decorate this room probably came from Lady Marjorie, whose brother, the Duke of Rutland, had commissioned the artist to paint a landscape view of his Derbyshire house, Haddon Hall, in 1933. Whistler had also decorated her sister, Lady Diana Cooper's London drawing room in 1935.

Whistler made his first visit to Plas Newydd at Easter 1936. The commission was agreed in April, and by July Whistler had produced a small, but detailed watercolour of the whole composition. He returned to Plas Newydd in September, when he sketched the outlines of the scheme onto the bare plaster. However, the mural itself was painted, not directly on the wall, but on canvas. To avoid distracting joins, a single, 58-foot length of material had to be specially woven in France. Whistler also had to rent a theatre workshop in Lambeth to accommodate it. His two assistants laid out the basic composition, but Whistler did all the detailed work himself. In late June 1937 the painted canvas was transported to Plas Newydd and carefully fixed to the wall. He made the final touches in August. His final bill came to a modest £1,000.

Below Whistler at work on his mural in the Dining Room

'I am going to paint the walls to make it appear, as though, when dining, one is sitting on a terrace overlooking a harbour. There is going to be a stone harbour bar running out with a light at the end rather like your exquisite one, and a little sea girt town on a promontory, and lots of ships and rocks and islands, etc., scattered all over the sea. At either end of the room I have planned a perspective pretending to be long arcaded rooms overlooking the sea again – as though one could walk into the picture, and on into another pavilion above the water.'

Rex Whistler to Mrs Hamlyn of Clovelly in Devon, 1936

'I've put an immense amount of detail into your little Town & it's now bristling with spires & domes & columns.'

Whistler to the 6th Marquess

The meaning of the mural

The landscape background was inspired by the mountains of Snowdonia, which are visible through the windows opposite. The panoramic harbour scene is more imaginary, but draws on memories of Mediterranean holidays, featuring a Venetian gondola and numerous classical and baroque buildings seen in Italy and Austria. Whistler's mastery of illusionistic perspective enabled him to unite the long wall smoothly with the arcades on the end walls, and the whole is bathed in a magical silvery light.

The mural is full of gentle humour and references to the Anglesey family. In the colonnade on the far wall he included Lady Marjorie's book and spectacles, together with her daughters' favourite pug dog and her son's baby cello. In the centre are Neptune's wet footprints, crown and trident, as if the sea-god had just stepped out of the water to join the family for supper. The figure holding the broom is a portrait of Whistler himself. The room was completed by painted coffering on the ceiling and (over the fireplaces on the end walls) trophies of arms painted in grisaille to resemble low-relief sculpture.

By common consent, the Plas Newydd mural is considered to be Whistler's masterpiece.

'All those days of fun and bathing and sunshine and moonlight and luxurious nights and enormous delicious meals … lovely, dear friends – and rows and rows of champagne cocktails.'

Rex Whistler to the 6th Marquess of Anglesey, 1938

Above The Whistler Dining Room

Left The silver-gilt *triumphal column* on the dining-table was presented to the 1st Marquess by the Prince Regent and officers of the Hussar Brigade in recognition of the 'Courage and Talent' he had shown during the Peninsular campaign of 1808. The column was designed and made by Paul Storr, who was an ancestor of Rex Whistler

THE GARDEN

Although the Menai Strait is exposed to Atlantic gales, it is warmed by the waters of the Gulf Stream, which allows a wide variety of tender plants including scented rhododendrons to flourish.

The world in one garden

At Plas Newydd you can enjoy exotic plants from across the planet – rhododendrons from the foothills of the Himalayas, shrubs from the Mediterranean in the Terrace Garden, and ferns and eucalyptus from the forests of Australia; and they are all set against the spectacular backdrop of Snowdonia. Here indeed you can travel around the world in 80 minutes.

Development of the garden

The earliest surviving planting probably dates from about the 1780s, when the 1st Earl of

Humphry Repton at Plas Newydd

Well-met by moonlight
Repton designed this Gothick-style conservatory, which would be 'seen from the library on one of those summer evenings, when such a pavilion would tempt us to walk out by moonlight, to enjoy the murmur of the waves, and the perfume of those plants which are most fragrant at that time.' Sadly, it was never built.

Uxbridge laid out new plantations with the advice of his friend and neighbour, Lt-Col William Peacocke of Plas Llanfair. In the 1790s he called in the leading garden designer Humphry Repton, who had already worked with the 1st Earl's architect, James Wyatt, at Sheffield Park. Repton praised the woodland walk 'so happily begun by the good taste of Lady Uxbridge', but was critical of some of the other changes that had already been made: 'They have proceeded too hastily at Plas Newydd in grubbing up hedges and pulling down cottages … where plantations ought to be encouraged to screen a bleak country'. Repton produced one of his famous Red Books, dated 1798–9 (now in the National Library of Wales), which contained designs for a cast-iron conservatory in an appropriate Gothick style. Sadly, it was never built, but a comparison of garden surveys made in 1798 and 1804 (illustrated) strongly suggests that most of his other proposals were carried out. Sycamores, beeches, oaks and limes, which are now mature, were planted to provide shelter from the prevailing winds and to screen out the public road. A new mile-long Grand Drive curved down to the house, which was hidden from view until the last moment for maximum dramatic effect. He also moved the home farm a mile to the south-west.

The 19th-century garden

The 1st Marquess made further extensive tree-planting after 1815, but the garden was neglected during the mid-19th century, when the house was tenanted. The 5th Marquess's lavish spending in the 1890s embraced the garden. He added a conservatory to the north of the house and laid out oval beds of gaudy annuals on the slope below.

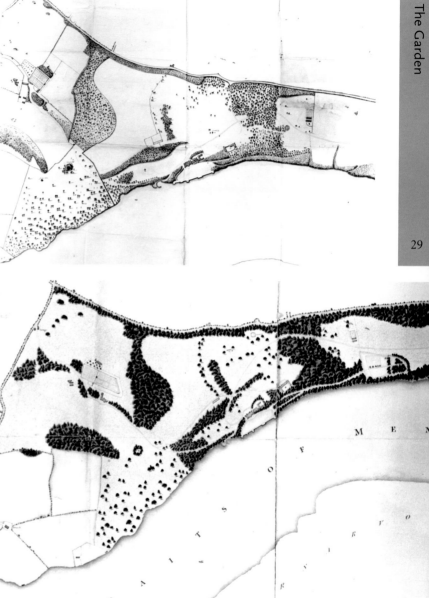

Top Plan of the garden in 1798

Above Plan of the garden in 1804 after Repton's planting proposals had been implemented

Opposite, above View of Plas Newydd from the south c.1800, detail of painting by John 'Warwick' Smith

Reviving the garden

In the 1920s and '30s, the 6th Marquess transformed the garden as part of his ambitious revival of the whole estate. He demolished the 5th Marquess's conservatory and on the same site created a terrace garden in the Italian style, with eight rectangular rose beds and formally clipped bay laurels and cypresses providing vertical accents. He carved a rhododendron garden out of Repton's woodlands ¾ of a mile to north-east of the house. He also brought camellias from the abandoned garden at Beaudesert, which were planted informally in the lawn to the south. In 1911 a dam on the River Aberbraint had given way, inadvertently creating a rock garden, which the Marquess planted with exotic trees and shrubs.

Inevitably, the 6th Marquess's rock garden and much of his other planting were neglected during the Second World War, and when the present Marquess inherited the estate in the austere climate of 1947, they had to be abandoned. The present Marquess simplified the Terrace Garden, removing the bay laurels and replacing most of the roses with four extensive beds, two recently replanted with blue agapanthus, and two with red and orange herbaceous plants. However, he was able to rescue and revive the Rhododendron Garden and in 1981 created a new Australasian arboretum of Eucalyptus and Southern Beech, which has overcome the threat of honey fungus and is now reaching maturity.

Left Lion's head fountain in the Terrace Garden

Opposite

Left Autumn colour in the garden

Right The Rhododendron Garden in bloom

Renewing the Rhododendron Garden

'As a wedding present Lord Aberconway presented us with some of what he called his 'thinnings' from Bodnant. For three successive seasons a lorry would arrive with these rhododendrons, some of them eight feet high. Accompanying them would be two gardeners equipped with shiningly polished spades for planting them.'

7th Marquess of Anglesey

TOUR OF THE GARDEN

5. 'WEST INDIES'

This is the main shrub garden to the south of the house, but no one seems to know how it got its name. It is laid out informally with large 'island' clumps of flowering shrubs in a 'sea' of grass. The beds of deciduous azaleas are usually at their floral height in late May. The old quarry in the south-east corner is planted with flowering cherries and camellias, some of which were brought from Beaudesert in the 1920s. The present Marquess planted the *Camellia williamsii* 'Donation' in the 1950s. Other highlights include the hydrangeas, Japanese maples (with their vivid autumnal colouring) and the Atlantic cedars. The oak surrounded by a circular bench is now 300–400 years old.

The magnolias are encouraged to grow to their full size and magnificence. The *Magnolia sargentiana robusta*, which was planted in 1953, is distinguished by its striking pink flowers. Look out also for the evergreen *M. grandiflora* 'Goliath', the rare *M. veitchii* and the free-flowering *M. wilsonii*.

Flowers to look out for through the seasons	
April	*Osmanthus delavayi*
May	Azaleas
July	Chilean Firebush
July–September	Hydrangeas
August-November	Eucryphias

Left Primulas in the Rhododendron Garden

6. THE LONG WALK

The Long Walk forms the southern boundary of 'West Indies'. It was planted with lilacs and laburnum in the 1930s to provide a shelter belt. These were cut down in the early 1950s, when the yews and the *Chamaecyparis pisifera* 'Squarrosa', which line the walk, had come to dominate.

From the bottom end of the walk there are fine views of Robert Stephenson's Britannia Bridge across the Menai Strait and of the Anglesey column, which is topped by Matthew Noble's 1860 statue of the 1st Marquess.

Right A colourful border of azaleas in 'West Indies'
Below Wild flowers are encouraged to flourish in 'West Indies'

7. THE ARBORETUM

This was originally laid out during the Second World War as an orchard, but by the late 1970s this had reached the end of its natural life. It was replanted as an Australasian garden filled with such trees as Eucalyptus and Southern Beech. In 1981 498 trees were planted in a geometric arrangement at five-metre intervals. Most survived the severe winter that followed and are now very well established. The grass beneath the trees is cut only two or three times a year to encourage wild flowers to self-seed.

8. THE DOCK, LANDING JETTY AND PORT

The 1st Marquess was the most distinguished British cavalry officer of his generation, but his family also has a long naval tradition and he himself loved sailing. A miniature harbour was built here in the early 19th century so that launches could come ashore from yachts anchored in the Strait. Those wishing to embark would wait in comfort in heated rooms nearby (not open to visitors).

Opposite The Italian Garden with the Menai Strait and Snowdonia beyond

9. THE TERRACE GARDEN

The present Marquess revived the formal Italian garden created by his father in the 1920s. Beyond the hedge at the southern end of the garden stands an Istrian stone statue of the messenger god Mercury.

10. LADY UXBRIDGE'S WALK

This shoreline walk links the house and the Terrace Garden with the Rhododendron Garden ¾ mile away to the north. In spring, the ground beneath the trees is carpeted with bluebells, wood anemones and daffodils.

11. THE RHODODENDRON GARDEN

Open only during the flowering season: usually late March–late May

The 6th Marquess created this six-acre glade in 1936 in the midst of the 18th-century Scots Fir woodland to the north of the house. Here he planted Himalayan rhododendron species such as *Rh. thomsonii*, *Rh.* 'Praecox', *Rh. fortuneii* and *Rh. montroseanum*. In the late 1940s the 7th Marquess added numerous cuttings from the Aberconways' famous rhododendron garden at Bodnant.

There are also beautiful mature magnolias, which have been allowed to grow to their full size, including *M. campbellii* and *M. veitchii*. Above the *Pieris forrestii* grows *Prunus serrulata* 'Ukon', which produces yellow flowers in May.

Below Eucalyptus trees in the Arboretum

THE MAKERS OF PLAS NEWYDD

PREHISTORY

The most obvious reminder that Plas Newydd has a 5,000-year history of human settlement is the cromlech (Neolithic burial mound) on the entrance lawn.

CELTS AND ROMANS

Anglesey was a stronghold of the Celtic Ordovices tribe and its Druid leaders, who resisted the Roman conquest of Britain in the 1st century AD. It took two bloody campaigns to subdue Mona (as the Romans called the island, which was already famous for its copper mines). In 60 AD Suetonius Paulinus confronted a Celtic army on the Menai Strait, as the Roman historian Tacitus described:

On the beach stood the adverse array, a serried mass of arms and men, with women flitting between the ranks. In the style of Furies, in robes of deathly black and with dishevelled hair, they brandished their torches; while a circle of Druids, lifting their hands to heaven and showering imprecations, struck the troops with such an awe at the extraordinary spectacle that, as though their limbs were paralysed, they exposed their bodies to wounds without an attempt at movement.

The Roman governor Agricola only finally conquered Anglesey in 79 AD, massacring the population and cutting down the groves of oak trees sacred to the Druids.

Left The cromlech

THE BAYLY FAMILY

In the 15th century, Plas Newydd belonged to the Griffith family, which owned huge tracts of north Wales, including Penrhyn (now also in the care of the National Trust). The estate passed by marriage in 1553 to the Bagenal family, and in the early 17th century, once again by marriage, to the Baylys, when Lewis Bayly wed Ann Bagenal.

Lewis Bayly (*c.*1575–1631) was chaplain to Henry, Prince of Wales, to whom he dedicated his *The Practise of Pietie*. Compiled from Bayly's rousing sermons, this was one of the key texts of Protestant devotion and had an important influence on the writings of John Bunyan. It was translated into Welsh in 1629 and was also very popular in 17th-century New England. Bayly was a man of strong opinions (he particularly abominated theatre-going) and when he was appointed Bishop of Bangor in 1616, he soon became embroiled in north Wales politics, falling out with several powerful local families. He was accused of bribery and failing to appoint Welsh-speaking clergy, but defended himself strongly by pointing out that he had paid for Bangor Cathedral's repair and supported a Welsh-Latin dictionary for the benefit of local preachers. He was buried in the cathedral in 1631.

Plas Newydd remained in the Bayly family for the next three generations, until 1737, when Sir Nicholas Bayly married Caroline Paget, who was the last in a line stretching back six generations to the Tudor diplomat and courtier, William Paget.

Right The title-page of Bishop Lewis Bayly's *The Practise of Pietie* (1618)

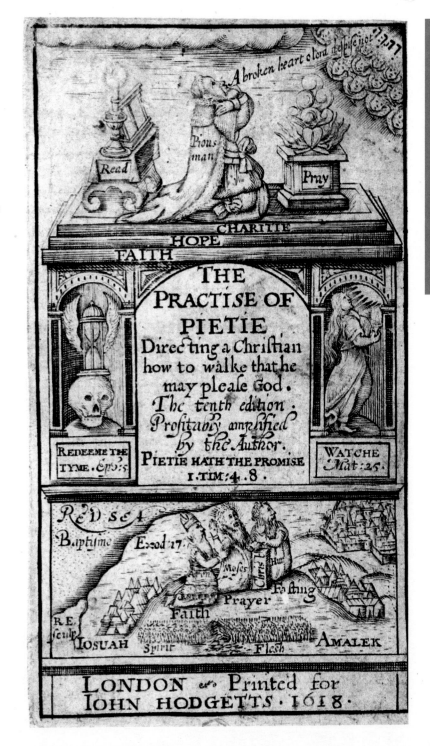

THE BARONS PAGET

The founder:
William, 1st Baron Paget (1505/6–63)

William Paget's origins were humble, but he received a good education at St Paul's school and Trinity Hall, Cambridge, where he came to the notice of the Master, Stephen Gardiner (later Lord Chancellor). He rose fast at Henry VIII's court, serving as secretary to three of Henry's queens. A talented linguist and rhetorician, he was trusted with sensitive diplomatic missions to the Continent, and ran the King's national intelligence service. He was particularly close to Henry during the latter's last days, and, with his old schoolfriend Anthony Denny, was the key figure in ensuring the smooth transition of power to 'Protector' Somerset, when the young Edward VI became king in 1547. His reward was to be made a knight of the Garter. However, Paget became increasingly disenchanted with Somerset's aggressive foreign policy, siding with the Earl of Warwick, when he led a coup. In 1549 William was raised to the peerage as Baron Paget of Beaudesert in Staffordshire, where he acquired a deer-park and large manor-house that had previously been the property of the bishops of Lichfield. But staying on top in the

William Paget's philosophy of life

'Fly the courte. Speke little. Care less. Desire nothing. Never earnest. In answer cold. Learne to spare. Spend in measure. Care for home. Pray often. Live better. And dye well.'

perilous world of the mid-16th-century English court was no easy matter. He was accused of corruption (and of being no gentleman), stripped of his Garter and imprisoned in the Tower of London.

Paget somehow survived into the reign of Queen Mary, who restored him to the Privy Council and used him to negotiate her marriage to Philip of Spain. Any friend of Mary was unlikely to be trusted by her successor, Elizabeth I, as Paget would have recognised. He stayed away from Elizabeth's court, pleading the genuine excuse of ill-health. This cautious, pragmatic diplomat kept his religious views to himself and sought above all to maintain peace and stability in England. He managed to die in his bed at the age of about 57, having amassed a fortune more or less honestly and founded a dynasty. He also proved a devoted husband to Anne Preston, 'my most obedient, wise, gentle and chaste wife', as he called her.

Above Beaudesert in Staffordshire was acquired by the 1st Baron and for 350 years was the Paget family's primary residence

Left Edward VI granted the 1st Baron his coat of arms with this royal patent dated 1553

Opposite William, 1st Baron Paget, the founder of the Paget family fortunes

The later Pagets and Baylys

Thomas, 3rd Baron Paget (*c.*1544–90) rebuilt Beaudesert on a very grand scale in the 1570s. He also abandoned his father's caution in religious matters, becoming by 1580 an overt Catholic – a very dangerous thing to be in Elizabethan England. When the Throckmorton Plot against Queen Elizabeth was unmasked in 1583, he fled to Paris to join his brother Charles, who had been openly working to place Mary Queen of Scots on the English throne. Thomas gave the excuse that he was seeking a cure for his gout, but no one believed him: his estates were confiscated, and he was convicted of treason in his absence. He died in exile in Brussels in 1590.

William, 4th Baron Paget (1572–1629) lived in the shadow of his father's treason, but after loyal military service on the Earl of Essex's Cadiz expedition, he eventually managed to regain the family estates, and in 1604 James I restored his title. However, he remained always short of money (he complained that he was 'the poorest man of his rank'), despite active involvement in such pioneering colonial projects as the Virginia Company, the Amazon River Company and the Bermudas Company. It was small recompense that the colonisers of the Somers Islands named a local tribe and fort after him.

In 1632 William, 5th Lord Paget (1609–78) married Lady Frances Rich, the daughter of a royal favourite, but he did not prosper at Charles I's court. When King and Parliament fell out, he found it difficult to know which side to back. A devout Presbyterian, he at first supported Parliament, but at the outbreak of war in 1642, he raised an infantry regiment that fought for Charles I at Edgehill. He gradually

Right *Caroline Paget*; by Enoch Seeman. Her marriage to Sir Nicholas Bayly in 1737 united the two families

became disillusioned with the King, but was appalled at his execution and supported the restoration of Charles II in 1660. His later years were clouded by ill-health and by money worries, which he tried to get the King to alleviate – without success.

William, 6th Lord Paget (1637–1713) was a radical Puritan who bore the deaths of two wives and two of his sons with stoicism. He backed James II's overthrow by William of

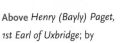

Orange, who appointed him as British ambassador in Vienna and Constantinople. Despite his short temper, he proved a talented diplomat, successfully chairing the Congress of Carlowitz, which brought peace to the Balkans in 1699.

In 1714 Henry, 7th Lord Paget (c.1663–1743) was also sent on a diplomat mission by the new King, George I, but he refused to go unless he was made an earl. The Queen promised him an earldom on his return, but he still refused to budge until the King finally conceded, creating him 1st Earl of Uxbridge. He was succeeded in 1743 by his grandson, who was also named Henry (1719–69) and is remembered for little beyond his extreme miserliness. Unwilling to share his fortune, he never married, so that on his death, the Paget barony passed to a distant cousin, Henry Bayly.

Henry Bayly (1744–1812) inherited not only an ancient title (in 1770, when in gratitude he changed his surname from Bayly to Paget), but also huge estates: in Somerset and Dorset in 1780 from his father's former steward, Peter Walter; and in Ireland and north Wales (including Plas Newydd) in 1782 from his father, Sir Nicholas Bayly. In all, his property comprised over 100,000 acres, which generated both agricultural rents and immense mineral wealth. Not surprisingly, he chose to be painted holding a sample of copper ore from Parys Mountain, which was then the largest copper mine in the world. He was ambitious for his children, but not for himself, preferring the quiet life of a loyal courtier in the Windsor entourage of George III. The King repaid his friendship by re-creating the Uxbridge earldom for him. Like the King, Uxbridge was a lover of music and a generous patron of promising young musicians. When he came to rebuild Plas Newydd in a hybrid Neo-classical-Gothick style in the 1780s, he turned the medieval Great Hall into a spacious Music Room. He also commissioned John Vardy junior to alter and extend Uxbridge House, the family's handsome London mansion off Piccadilly. (The house was given up in the 1850s, but still stands.)

Above Henry (Bayly) Paget, 1st Earl of Uxbridge; by George Romney

Left Sir Nicholas Bayly; by Enoch Seeman

'ONE-LEG': HENRY, 1st MARQUESS OF ANGLESEY (1768-1854)

The most famous member of the family began life as Henry William Bayly and ended it as a Paget, a field marshal and a marquess. His distinguished military career spanned the Napoleonic Wars.

In 1792, soon after war broke out, he raised an infantry regiment from among his father's tenants, whom he led into battle during the 1794 Flanders campaign. Something of a dandy, he transferred to the more glamorous world of the cavalry, being given command of the 7th Light Dragoons (later Queen's Own Hussars) in 1797. For the rest of his long career, he remained devoted to the 7th, which he turned into one of the crack regiments in the British Army. (He wears its uniform in the two full-length portraits in the Music Room.)

In the Spanish Peninsula in 1808, he successfully covered Sir John Moore's famous retreat to Corunna. He managed to execute this most complex of military manoeuvres despite being able to muster only five cavalry regiments to the enemy's thirteen.

His private life was almost as fraught. In 1810 he left his wife Caroline to elope with Charlotte Wellesley, the sister-in-law of the future Duke of Wellington, who was commanding British forces in Spain. Charlotte's brother challenged Henry Paget (as he had become) to a duel. Both combatants survived the encounter, but divorce from Caroline cost Paget £55,000 and many years' estrangement from Wellington. His new wife, Charlotte, who bore him ten more children, was also excluded from polite society.

Left Henry, 1st Marquess of Anglesey was a man of boundless courage, energy and self-confidence. He was painted by Sir Thomas Lawrence as colonel of his beloved 7th Light Dragoons

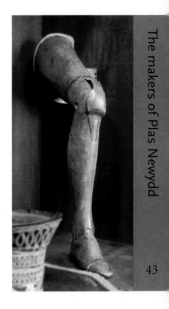

'A tall, well-made man; wild, martial face, high forehead, with a large hawk's nose, which makes a small, deep angle where it joins the forehead. A great deal of ease in his manners.'

Baron Stockmar on the 1st Marquess, 1816

Paget's military career reached its bloody climax at the battle of Waterloo in 1815. By now Lord Uxbridge and second-in-command to Wellington, he led the allied cavalry and horse artillery. At a key point in the battle, he led a charge by two brigades of heavy cavalry, who routed a much larger French force. He remained in the thick of the action, having eight or nine horses shot from under him, until late in the day, when his right knee was smashed by grapeshot. 'By God, sir, I've lost my leg!' he is said to have exclaimed to the nearby Wellington, who replied, 'By God, sir, so you have!' before coolly returning his telescope to his eye and continuing to observe the progress of the battle. He endured the amputation of his leg at the knee with equal stoicism and for the rest of his life wore an ingenious articulated leg (one version of which was designed for riding, and another for walking).

Paget was made a marquess by the grateful Prince Regent, but nothing in his later years matched the glory of Waterloo. In 1828 he served as lord lieutenant of Ireland in Wellington's Tory government, but fell out with his old commander over Catholic emancipation (which he supported) and was called home. Never a party man, he was happy to return to Ireland two years later in Earl Grey's Whig administration, during which he put in place a national education system for Ireland. The Marquess remained in government well into his eighties, having long ago been reconciled with Wellington.

The 1st Marquess lived mostly at Uxbridge House in London and Beaudesert, for which he bought handsome modern furniture from the Lancaster firm of Gillows. He left relatively little impression on Plas Newydd, which was rented out for much of the early 19th century.

Above The artificial 'Anglesey leg' is articulated at the knee, ankle and toe joints

Left Uxbridge's shattered leg was amputated without anaesthetic. 'He never moved or complained: no one even held his hand. He said once perfectly calmly that he thought the instrument was not very sharp'

THE 1st MARQUESS'S CHILDREN

The 1st Marquess had no fewer than eighteen children by his two wives and 73 grandchildren. So Pagets were commonplace in Victorian high society.

The Marquess's favourite son was Clarence, who rose to be a vice-admiral, but had few opportunities to shine in battle in the more peaceful, post-Waterloo world. He was more influential representing the admiralty in the House of Commons, where he was a powerful advocate of the new ironclad battleships. The Marquess's *least* favourite son was the spendthrift Lord William Paget, who caused his father endless difficulties (see p.13).

The Marquess's eldest son, Henry (later 2nd Marquess), was Lord Chamberlain to Queen Victoria, but continued to behave like a Regency rake of the previous era. Lord Alfred Paget was also a member of the royal household, serving the young Queen from 1837 as a devoted equerry: both he and his dog (a retriever named Mrs Bumps) wore portrait miniatures of Victoria round their necks. Prince Albert was less enamoured of Lord Alfred and the many other Pagets at court, whom he is said to have likened to 'a plague of locusts'. Lord George Paget upheld the Paget military tradition well into the Victorian age. In the Crimean War, he served as second-in-command of the Light Cavalry, surviving the infamous Charge of the Light Brigade. He was accompanied on campaign by his beautiful young wife Agnes ('the belle of the Crimea', according to the photographer Roger Fenton).

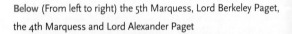

Below Lord Uxbridge (later 2nd Marquess) is shown riding the grey horse behind the young Queen Victoria in Windsor Great Park

Below (From left to right) the 5th Marquess, Lord Berkeley Paget, the 4th Marquess and Lord Alexander Paget

THE 3rd AND 4th MARQUESSES

The 2nd Marquess was succeeded (as 3rd Marquess) in 1869 by his unmarried eldest son, and in 1889 (as 4th Marquess) by his second son. Confusingly, these half-brothers were both christened Henry. Neither lived at Plas Newydd and neither left much mark on the place.

THE DANCING MARQUESS

Henry Cyril Paget was the only son of the 4th Marquess's second wife, Blanche, but gossip had it that his father was actually a French actor, Benoit Coquelin. Certainly, after his mother died in 1877, he was brought up in France by Coquelin's sister. A lonely child, he became fascinated by all things theatrical. His coming-of-age in June 1896 was marked at Plas Newydd by lavish celebrations, which drew thousands of wellwishers. In 1898 he married his cousin Lilian, who was the daughter of Lady Florence Paget, the notorious 'Pocket Venus' (see p.14). Later the same year, he inherited the family estate and the substantial fortune that came with it. He was now able to indulge his passion for jewellery to the full. He established the Polish jeweller Morris Wartski in a shop in Llandudno to supply his growing obsession. Only the best would do, which included a magnificent emerald necklace that had once belonged to Marie Antoinette. Fashion statement turned to fetish, as Lilian was obliged to undress and lie motionless while he covered her naked body with a glittering array of precious gems. Perhaps not surprisingly, the marriage was dissolved in 1900.

The 5th Marquess returned to his first love, amateur theatricals, converting the chapel at Plas Newydd into the 'Gaiety Theatre'. Decorated in blue and white, its design was based on the Paris theatre used by Sarah Bernhardt. The first production, in 1901, was of *Aladdin*, in which the Marquess played Pekoe, the grand vizier's son, dressed in exotic, jewel-encrusted robes. His speciality was the solo 'Butterfly Dance', at the end of which he distributed photographs of himself in costume to the bemused audience.

The inevitable reckoning came in June 1904, when his trustees intervened to halt his reckless spending. By this stage, his debts had reached the astonishing figure of £544,000, most of which was due to jewellers. 40 days of sales followed, which included the Marquess's pet dogs together with their silk jackets embroidered in silver thread with his coat of arms. He took refuge in the Hôtel Royale in Monte Carlo, where he died with his estranged wife at his side in 1905.

45

'As a sort of apparition he was quite unforgettable – a tall, elegant and bejewelled creature, with wavering, elegant gestures, reminding one rather of an Aubrey Beardsley illustration come to life.'

Clough Williams Ellis on the 5th Marquess

THE 20TH CENTURY

The 6th Marquess of Anglesey

The 5th Marquess had no children so that the title and what was left of the estate passed in 1905 to his cousin Charles, who had never expected to inherit. The 6th Marquess fought in the First World War, but was obliged to give up a promising army career to take on this challenge. Over the next half-century, he not only rescued Plas Newydd, but thoroughly reinvigorated the place with the vital support of his wife, Lady Marjorie Manners, who was the daughter of the 8th Duke of Rutland and a talented amateur artist. However, he had first to make some difficult decisions. The most important was to give up the Pagets' ancestral home at Beaudesert. He put the house on the market in 1920, but it failed to find a buyer, and it was not until 1935 that it was eventually sold for scrap and demolished. The shell realised only £800, but at least the salvaged Tudor bricks were put to good use in repairing St James's Palace in London.

The Angleseys preserved Plas Newydd's hybrid Neo-classical-cum-Gothick character, while at the same time transforming it into one of the most comfortable country houses in Britain. For the first time in two centuries, Plas Newydd was the family's primary residence. Here also the

Angleseys revived the British tradition of country house patronage, commissioning Rex Whistler to paint the famous Dining Room mural. The 6th Marquess also continued the long family tradition of royal service as Lord Chamberlain to Queen Mary for 22 years.

During the Second World War, Plas Newydd was used as an officer-training school and took in a party of primary school children evacuated from Liverpool. Lady Anglesey was in her element, as a friend recalled: 'When Marjorie went for one of her brisk walks in the park or on the sea shore in the afternoon, as

Top right Charles, 6th Marquess of Anglesey, who modernised Plas Newydd in the 1930s; painted by Rex Whistler

Right Lady Marjorie Manners, Marchioness of Anglesey; bust by William Reid Dick

often as not she was attended by a little fringe of children trotting beside her. She talked to them exactly as if they saw and understood things as she did.' Another remembered her 'singing half a song, darting into the kitchen to fetch the tea, pouring out encouragement on one and all'.

The 7th Marquess of Anglesey

The 7th Marquess inherited Plas Newydd from his father in 1947. A distinguished military historian, he is the author of a biography of the 1st Marquess and an eight-volume history of the British Cavalry. He has also served on many public bodies concerned with the arts and historic buildings in Wales and beyond, including the National Museum of Wales, the Historic Buildings Council for Wales and the National Heritage Memorial Fund. His wife Shirley is the daughter of the novelist Charles Morgan and has been Chairman of the National Federation of Women's Institutes, the Welsh Arts Council and the Broadcasting Complaints Commission, and Vice-Chairman of the Museums and Galleries Commission. She was appointed DBE in 1983 and LVO in 1993. In 1976 the 7th Marquess generously gave Plas Newydd and 68 hectares (169 acres) of surrounding garden and woodland, including one and a half miles of the Menai Strait coastline, to the National Trust. The Angleseys continue to live at Plas Newydd, maintaining a family connection that is now over five centuries old.

Top left The 7th Marquess's sisters
Left The 7th Marquess, who is a distinguished military historian, in his library

The Bayly and Paget Families

Owners of Plas Newydd are shown in Capitals
* Indicates a portrait in the house

Gwilym ap Gruffydd = Morfudd, dau. of Goronwy
(d.1431) | Fychan of Penmynydd

William, 1st Baron Paget de = Anne Preston
Beaudesert* (1505/6–63) | (d.1589) m.1530

Sir Nicholas Bagenal, Kt = Ellen Griffith of
(1510?–90) | Penrhyn (d.1573)

Henry, 2nd Baron Paget = Katherine Knyvett
(d.1568) | (d.1622) m.1560

Thomas, 3rd Baron Paget = Nazareth Newton*
(1544–89) | m.1565

Sir Henry Bagenal, Kt (1556–98) = Eleanor Savage

William, 4th Baron Paget (1572–1629) = Lettice Knollys

Lewis Bayly, Bishop of = Anne Bagenal
Bangor (1573?–1631) | (d.c.1623)

William, 5th Baron Paget = Lady Frances Rich
(1609–78) | (d.1672) m.1632

Nicholas Bayly (1620?–89) = Anne (Jane?) Hall

William, 6th Baron Paget = Frances Pierrepoint
(1637–1713) | (d.1681) m.1661

Henry Paget = Mary O'Rorke
m.1684

Sir Edward Bayly 1st Bt = Dorothy Lambert
(d.1741) | (d.1745) m.1708

Henry, 7th Baron Paget = Mary Catesby (d.1734)
1st Earl of Uxbridge* | m.1685
(c.1663–1743)

Brig.-Gen Thomas = Mary Whitcombe
Paget* (d.1741) | (d.1741)

Thomas Catesby, Lord = Lady Elizabeth Egerton
Paget (1689–1742) | (d.1736) m.1718

Josias de Robillard Seigneur = Maria de la Rochefoucauld (d.1730)
de Champagné (d.1689) | g/dau. of Charles, Duc de la Rochefoucauld

Henry, 8th Baron Paget, 2nd Earl of Uxbridge (1719–69)

Josias de Champagné (1673–1737) = Lady Jane Forbes, dau. of 2nd Earl of
Granard (d.1760)

Sir Nicholas Bayly, = Caroline Paget*
2nd Bt* (1709–82) | (d.1766) m.1737

Arthur Champagné, Dean of = Marianne Hamon
Clanmacnoise (1714–1800) | (d.1784)